the TASTE *of* WATER

~~~~~

The Taste of Water
Frank Ledwell

The Acorn Press
Charlottetown
2006

The Taste of Water © 2006 by Frank Ledwell
ISBN 1-894838-25-4

Editing by Jane Ledwell
Cover painting by Danny Ledwell
Author Photo by John Sylvester
Design by Matthew MacKay
Printing by Hignell Book Printing

Canada Council   **Conseil des Arts**
for the Arts   **du Canada**

We acknowledge the financial support of the Government of Canada through the Book Publishing Industry Development Program (BPIDP) for our publishing activities. We also acknowledge the support of the Canada Council for the Arts which last year invested $20.0 million in writing and publishing throughout Canada.

Library and Archives Canada Cataloguing in Publication

Ledwell, Frank J., 1930–

    The taste of water / Frank Ledwell.

Poems.

ISBN 1-894838-25-4

    I. Title.

PS8573.E3469T38 2006   C811'.54   C2006-906021-5

The Acorn Press
P.O. Box 22024
Charlottetown, PE C1A 9J2
www.acornpresscanada.com

for Anna Sophia

You always told me
to remember stories
about our village;
to remember the songs
that carry the legends
of our land;
to remember the faces
of the old people,
for in them is our history.
Isn't that so?

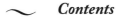 ***Contents***

Leaving Home

How bonded we all were there,
nine packed into our
small green dining room.
Mother bearing dinner from the kitchen
range, insisting on grace
before serving. Father, a hungry
railway man — eight potatoes for him —
gives his dessert to his youngest
sitting to his left. He talks of heroes
from his early days in Souris —
Mother, of the new mat design
in her frame. Tales of high jinks
played at school — warnings not
to go too far.

Then cutting the cards to see
who'd do the dishes — high, wash;
low, dry. The round table cleared
for homework in the light
of the Aladdin lamp. Then the beads,
a decade for each of the older ones —
the younger ones getting giddy —
more admonitions. Going off
to unheated bedrooms overhead —
two to a bed under heavy woolen
Condon's blankets, sharing body

warmth, watching breath clouds
dissipate before blowing
out the lamp. Frost making angel
wings on the window panes.

One by one going off to college
and on to other lives. The house
now closed upon itself. The
parents gone to God, the table
sold at auction. The ceiling
plaster of that little dining room,
having lost its bond, clutters the floor.

This Is What I Remember

What I remember is the smell of birchwood
burning in the kitchen range, and the stories
of the once upon a time when horses ran back
into burning barns and forerunners told of death,
of a dog wailing all night before a tragedy
in the community, a roughbox seen at a gate,
a spirit appearing, a ghost ship, a cloven hoof.

What I remember is Chingachcook, the Last
of the Mohicans, the Little Match Girl, the Happy
Prince, being read or told at the oil-clothed table
beside the kitchen range — the smell of the kerosene lamp
at night. What I remember are the songs, "I'm a comin'
I'm a comin' for my head I bendin' low," and "Thought
he was a goner, but the cat came back because he
couldn't stay away." And evenings of little Paul
on the fiddle and my mother at the piano
and reels and rounds of "Pigeon at the Gatepost"
and "Nellie in the Cornfield" and "Pop Goes the Weasel."

And I remember the salt cod and blue potatoes,
and the fresh side-bacon from the recent-killed pig
sizzling in the pan, before the rest of the pork
would be salted down for the winter, and the
homemade beans this Saturday night. I remember
thinking: this is how it should be. This is how
it should be all the time — all of us wrapped up

together in the ſtories and in the music, connected
and bound by what brings us together. I remember
this because it was back in the once upon a time
when we shared each other's ſtories, and the woodſtove
range and kitchen table were our common ground.

And then I realized what I think I always knew:
that ſtorytelling has never really left us, with
our mass media and mobility. There is always
someone coming along with a ſtory to tell, whether
funny or sad, true or out of the imagination —
filling the room, sweeping over the liſteners like aromatic
pipe smoke, rippling like brook water over the rocks,
catching up the hearers in its flow. People recognizing
themselves in the ſtory, or creating ſtories of their own,
right then and there while they liſten. "I remember
the time—" "Oh yes," they will say, "and I remember,
too, but it was another time — my time, my place,
my ſtory." A memory recollected, memory
believing, and the spirit of the spoken word taking hold.

And I remember, as I know you do, too, how
ſtories swirled through my veins, in my blood, in my bones,
pulsing, soaring — sometimes laughing,
sometimes crying — the shared love of family,
of community, of common culture. This is what
I remember and what I hope you remember, too.

The Sweater

You dragged your feet when you went out...
          — Ezra Pound, "The River Merchant's Wife: A Letter"

I was a red-haired Scottish lass.
I grew up on the farm in Bear River.
You came by my gate in your half-ton.
I had our cream can for pick-up.
You stopped and asked me to come
to the dance in Naufrage.
You had your fisherman's rubber
boots on. I said yes.

You came around every day
 after stacking your traps.
I said I'm a good knitter.
"Trap heads?" you asked.
"No, sweaters, mitts, and socks."
We married in months.
I was already growing with child.

I knitted you a cable sweater
to keep you warm on the boat.
Other wives did the same, each
sweater a pattern like a
fingerprint. I made you
thick fisherman's mitts for hauling

the traplines. Our boy was born
before the opening day.

The race to the grounds paid
no mind to the gathering clouds
to the weſt, the ſtorm coming on
too faſt. Five boats didn't return.

For weeks I walked the rain-swept
shores, waiting for you to come home.
I found your sweater wet in the sand.
I found you so I could put you
and my heart to reſt.

Brothers Fishing at MacLeod's Pond

In the spillway below the sawmill
we see the water swirl.
We come with bamboo poles, a basket,
spare hooks, sinkers, two cans
of worms. My brother collects twigs
and builds a fire. "You catch the fish.
Bill makes little fires," our father
always said. "He's not got the patience."

I trained with Uncle Gus who'd stay
until he'd have to turn on his
half-ton's headlights to see the hole.
"The big ones come to the light,"
he'd whisper, waking the already
sleeping boy when he got back to the cab.
Whether true or another fish story,
he always snagged his limit.

I run a barbed hook through
a wriggling night crawler, let out
a line, sit down upon a discarded
millstone, and wait.

Country School

The taste of water at our one-room school
was of Pine Brook that flowed
down under the Bay's thick ice,
our bucket lowered into a deeper hole
where smelts would later school
in their spring run, hauled up, carried up
the snowy bank into the porch to sit,
wooden-lid-covered, on its special ledge
among the coats and boots. I dippered up
my water with a small tin cup
that swung from a nail beside.
Unschooled about germs,
I drank; I tasted snow and arithmetic.

Back Home

In winter the farms doze,
their tillage deep in snow —
the bay a mirror
against skate cuts, dim fish
schooling up under the ice
towards smelt nets. We haul
enough for supper and fetch
in kindling for Mother,
carrying her seventh. The fire
rubs us with warmth and
the windows go beaded with frost.
We kneel for evening Rosary
before our own kind of hibernation.

The Old Homestead

They go back to where they began, climbing
backwards down the family tree, reclaiming
the family home. They begin by peeling
back the layers of wallpaper that overlay
the walls. They are armed with brushes, hot
water, scrapers. Grandma papered everything
from porch to attic. She made a paste of flour
and water to hold her patterns firm. The walls
were murescoed when she came here first:
pinks and pale greens, like Van Gogh's bedroom —
her first act to cover their drab. Floral
patterns for each room; she liked subtle yellows,
blues, and browns, smoky now from coal stoves
in the house. Later years brought country scenes
to the living rooms, teapots and kettles to the kitchen,
horses rampant in the halls, bright diamonds and
circles for the children's rooms. Tearing away
pages of family history. At each layer another
decade comes alive — unrolling the family map.
The room where their own mother and her sister
slept together, breathing out of the shadows.
The spare room where each of the seven was born,
now deaf to the cries of birth. Stubborn places
where oil lamps set too close left singes.
The parlour paper behind the piano still unfaded —

there since '21 — echoes a room full of people
on Sunday visits. Up to where northern lights
danced on the boys' dorm walls in winter —
whispering and wondering about ghosts and goblins,
until warned to shush. In the slant-walled
parents' room, hardest to do, faded roses
come up. Each layer unpeeled redeems another memory:
of Grandma sprinkling rooms with holy water
in thunder storms, fish on Fridays, children
gone now to infirmity who once slid down
banisters. All this and much more in the nooks
and crannies to tell the way it was.
The paper rustles when they fold it all away.

Home from the Dance

Yez come traipsin' in from the shindig
At a quarter after two
Like a coupla' blatherin' eejets
To yer momma's worryin' rue.

Yez were in cahoots, were yez,
When the fight was a settoo,
Galoots sp'ilin' fer conniptions,
Itchin' fer a wingdang-do?

Vamoose y'two scalawags,
Skedaddle both of yez.
Hotfoot it t'yer beds now —
Enuf of bein' buckaroos.

I'll put the kibosh t'yer shenigans
At six when I git yez up,
 so hornswoggle yer palaver
'Fore y'git me dander up.

Literacy

We sit at the kitchen table
a storybook between us.
Your gnarled finger points to words.
You know housework for others —
how it works, scrubbing floors,
dusting, laundering, polishing.
I know this thing called reading.
We've worked for weeks now
getting some sounds down.
You know words from your life:
work, family, house, car, neighbours —
that last the hardest,
nay-nay-nay, bores-bores.
Then words begin to come together:
The book, *Little Red Riding Hood*, your first.
Bedtime stories to read for grandchildren
you couldn't do for your own, recipes,
phone books, places you'd like to visit.
You only go so far. I'll still do
your tax forms for you every April.

John James MacKinnon's Farm

At twelve, I worked John James' farm
while he went off to build Morell Co-op's store.
A carpenter and a farmer, he had the former's eye
for keeping a neat place: a pearl grey home
and a hip-roofed barn atop the Pine Brook hill.
He knew each beam and rafter as it gave shape
to a fine-lined building. The sky was always blue
that summer, as I remember it. Mowing hay
with a team of horses as skittish as himself:
he had a nervous tic and made small
spitting sounds with his mouth, as if getting rid
of pits. His animals seemed to catch his edginess.

Windrowing and coiling the hay was easiest,
hoisting it on the hayfork and stowing in the loft,
the hardest — dusty work. Hoeing turnips tedious,
hilling potatoes a joy, the rows as straight as set
to a level. My mind wandered to my friends
swimming in the Bay. I watched the grain grow
tall and, small for my age, hoped for a similar
rapid growth. A hail storm flattened it, but later
the grain returned upright; the crops were good:
the Green Mountains monstrous, the turnips
without brown heart, the clay cellar stocked.
John James, pleased, had no trouble paying me $2.50 a day.
He had his dreams and I had mine.

Country Boys

Two boys on the brink of knowing who they are
and who they would become shake off their shoes'
red clay and set forth. "Education is the key,"
their parents said who, themselves, were denied
beyond grade school.

Both boys had dreamt the Canadian dream of making it
to the NHL, or trying out, and, if not, being
sports writers, to satisfy their youthful passion,
listening to French-language broadcasts
of Canadiens' games on CHNC New Carlisle.

Live-in college next where learning and the rule
went hand in hand: the classics, Latin, French,
history, literature, and philosophy, but still
not finding selves, not future vision clear.

Writing Latinate prose at college, not exactly
a good schooling for sports-scribe style.
One, undaunted, scored goals for the college team
and became an award-winning sports columnist;
the other, tried the church and ended up a teacher —
wrote poems and stories on the side.

Both plied their art to bring the dreams of others
to fulfillment: to read the times, to dare
to challenge, to look through the soft underbelly
of things, realizing in the end that becoming
is a lifelong search — as continuous as the shining stars:
we cannot place exactly who we are.

Blueberry Picking

Summer came as it always did
and after haying was blueberry time:
a two-mile walk along the dusty
Cardigan road to our favourite barren.
Mary Donald Angus was kind enough to let us
pick there; others more scroogy about their fields.
These were the sounds of our 1941 season:
the harvest flies' excited song. Then the Harvard
Trainers flying low overhead, as yellow as wasps
and, it being wartime, as threatening. We'd cover
our heads as they swept low in mock strafing exercises.
My brother, the disciplinarian, inspecting my berries
lest I have leaves and unripe ones among them;
urging me to pick faster, to keep up. Lunchtime
was best. A bubbling spring in the nearest bush
kept our Rawleigh's lime juice cold, and
the brookside sand, our peanut butter sandwiches cool.
That day, if we picked more than needed for home,
we could sell the extra at the village store
for six cents a pound. One pound bought a Sweet Marie
chocolate bar or a Seaman's pop — leaving one cent
change with which, if we were so daring, we could buy
a Player's cigarette. ("For Dad," we'd tell the storekeeper.)
"Them are the cleanest berries I got all day,"

the storekeeper'd say. "And by the look of yer mouths
y'ate yer share too." The berries were so plentiful
they burned images into my eyes; I could still replay
in bed at night — blankets of blue. I could still hear
crickets filling the silence, rubbing their legs,
making mating calls. My camera eyes return
to document another cherished memory.

Jean Finding Things

Jean keeps her eyes open.
She's the first to espy
a four-leaf clover on the lawn,
a nighthawk twittering in the sky,
a piping plover egg along the beach,
pebble gems polished in the tides.
Quick things: a cupboard mouse,
a dime's glint in the grass,
a hermit crab hidden in the rocks.
All sorts of lost stuff
about the house: needles, specs, socks;
a son's thistle splinter others cannot spot.
"Look, there it is," she says, far easier than not.

Nature Walk

Forty-seven acres of woods at Fortune Bridge.
Potato fields and a secondary road to the west; a run down
to a bird sanctuary riverfront to the north; a clearcutting saw
on a neighbouring stand of woodland to the east.

We walk through with Lorne, a wheelwright, third-generation owner
of the property. We can't afford to buy, but welcome the tour.
Lorne hops like a leprechaun over knolls,
"They were created by Mi'kmaqs storing clam shells there
in the early days — midden mounds, they're called," he says.

"Back in the days when we built carriages and driving sleighs
and heavy wagon wheels here, we got our lumber from the Dixons
up in the Baltic. A lot of it was first-growth yellow birch — rock hard."

"It never grew here in our woods." He points to maple,
white birch, spruce, and var, more common fare to the Island.
We spot the occasional ash and beech. "My father's driving wagons
were as common on the Island as cars are now. When he died,
I took over, but their days were done.

"I had a contract for a whole batch of heavy wagon wheels
for the Magdalenes in '51. Then I wrecked my car
and smashed my leg goin' to a dance at the Bay —
drunk as arse. I was on crutches for two years, but I got
those wheels done for them. A man's only as good as his word."

Our footsteps sink in the rich forest bed of mosses and plush
organic growth. We name five species of fern, cowslips,
pigeon berries, and lady's slipper, their blossoms
gone since spring. "There's this great horned owl out here.
Y'oughta see his wingspan. Too bad he's not around today."

He is enough owl for our imaginations.
"If I sold these forty-seven acres and the new owner laid
this forest flat, I'd be back to guzzle him."

John of the Island

It is hard to say what this Island means to others.
A huge map in British Columbia's Tourism Information Centres
does not show it —
an empty space in the Gulf of St. Lawrence.

It is the place of my birth,
the world of my childhood —
rocking in the sea, a cradle.
I grew out of it like a spruce sapling —
rooted — growing slowly at first,
then tall and sturdy, withstanding
the on-shore winds. Here I am at home.
I know every curve in the road.
I know the red back roads
and the green hills. It is the red
and green I love and the salt sea
scent in the ocean air.
I do not need a map to tell me
I am here. I call each house by name.
Last year this field grew potatoes,
this year grain. I say "G'day"
to every person in the malls. I know
their parents, where they're from
and where they're going. I can
tell you where to find the biggest

trout in every brook. I have felt
the pain of low prices for fish
and potatoes, and the joy of a good
ceilidh — toe-tapping music and
family gatherings. Here I am at home.
I hope my body will sink down here.
I do not need a map.

The Skipper

He came in on high tide at Souris
at the age of forty-two, thirty years
under sail behind him. Home is the sailor.

He'd been a twelve-year-old lad forking caplin
in Placentia Bay when he boarded the first
boat out of port. The rhythm of the ocean

a lap-call, the smell of salt in the nostrils
trimming the mainsail in the Falklands to buck
the winds round the Horn, a ship under
his own command at twenty-one.

Then back to Gloucester, Mass., to meet
an Island girl who never once handlined cod
though she grew up three miles from the Gulf shore
on the North Side of the Island.

From Gloucester to Souris, a short run
in the lee of the land, to retire from the spray
and raise a brood on a farm on the Line Road:
five girls and two boys on fifty acres.

Born on the Rock and bred on the waters,
he knew little of farming. If it was cod
he could sow in the rows, he'd get a grand crop.

Potatoes, now, they were another thing: he never
heard of cutting sets, just filleting sole. The eye
of the cobbler beguiled him, and bluestone
for blight, a mystery.

Grandmother, being away as she was
for years as a housemaid in Boston,
had long forgot the way to hoe turnips.
Savings from the sea had to tide them over
till the sons were of age to farm.

The skipper, old, now, still yearns for the sea-dreaming
of nights in Cathay — tapping the alarm clock for a barometer,
going out at night to read Polaris, the guiding star.
While grandma, we're told, is just glad enough
to be back home on the Island.

Sara Murphy's Quilt

In the grey afternoon, the shore winds astir,
Sara Murphy sat at her quilting frame
awaiting the arrival of Bridget, Florence, and Mary Mac
to come to her bee — she'd already set a pot of tea
on the back of the range, and got out the biscuits
and blueberry jam.

Commotion in the porch signalled their arrival.
"Beastly wind," they said. "No boats off shore today."
The patches were already laid out on the quilt —
The fabrics cut out from piles of rags sent home
from away, worn in places to a frazzle
but too expensive and too pretty to throw out.

"Come on in," said Sara, her Woolworth's glasses
for sewing already on her nose.
"I've been waiting for you the while."
It was an afternoon for talking while they worked
with their needles, deft fingers with decades
of experience. Bridget had been bedridden
with the grippe for weeks and was, she said,
"'Way behind on the goin's on."

Florence and Mary Mac were only too eager
to fill her in on who's in the family way,
on what was said about her at the last

Women's Institute meeting, and on the spat
between Angus and Jenny from the back road.
"I know nothing but good of Jenny," Sara said.
"Well then, let's talk about someone else," said Mary Mac.

And so, they went on to Johnny Roddie's horse
having the heaves and not being able to haul
Irish moss from the shore anymore, and about
how Pete Simon has got too old to play
the fiddle at dances in the parish hall this year.
"You don't say, now. Who will take his place?"
"We'll have to go outside the village for a fiddler."
"A shame it is. A cryin' shame."

The quilt took shape: the reds as striking
as the Island loam, the middle squares green
and gold farm fields, the shoreline around the edges
as light-inflected blue as the shore they lived beside,
each woman filled with the desire to own her share
of every square, to be a part of it.

"Sure now, 'tis like the Island itself," said Florence.
"Good enough to hang on the parlour wall," said Mary Mac.
"Or to lay it down by the edge of the shore," said Bridget.
"Oh no," said Sara, "it will be for comforting and
snuggling with my John."
Time then for tea and biscuits and jam.

Lasagna, April '06

"You never can tell who might pop in.
You've gotta have something in the freezer,"
she said. She's a soft touch for Tupperware.
Keeping each container filled and labelled
with strips of masking tape. Each dated,
a library of foods for drop-in visitors.

They usually stay for a bite to eat,
small price to pay for a huge extended family.
Lasagna, spaghetti sauce, meatballs, sweet
and sour ribs, soya chicken, soup stocks,
cranberries, raspberries, strawberries, blueberries.
Ten years ago she bought a second freezer
for the overflow of breads, biscuits, muffins and buns.
Ginger cookies are great right out of the freezer:
more snap to them. More and more tape labels,
keeping the 3M folks in business.
Not to mention Tupperware.
Sometimes they will say, "We'll just have
a cup of tea and one of your lovely squares."
"You'll have to wait until they thaw out.
You can stay that long?" she inquires.
They stay: Lemon squares, September '05. The tea
is hot, the squares sweet and tangy. They decide

to stay on for mealtime: Lasagna, April '06,
and, if they want, prebaked frozen apple pie: October '05.
The library shelves will be refilled next day.
Only the label date will change.

Under This Road, What Lies?

To your immediate right, on the turn of the road
at Stukeley where a churchbell was found in a field
is a graveyard where the first Presbyterian
minister on the Island, Rev. Peter Gordon, is buried —
a marked headstone. But, under the paved curve
of the road lies a Mi'kmaq burying ground,
long since forgotten except by those who know
it to be there.

In the pavement's subgrade
you will find no monuments.
None of the dead here comes dressed
in a coffin. Under the bulldozer's blade
they were unearthed on the ground —
not ceremoniously as with an archaeologist's
spade and brush: a pearl of glass which once
hung around someone's neck, totems etched
on bedrock, flint shards and arrowheads,
a fishing spear, some skulls and assorted
bones — then re-interred falling back
into the shadows.

Now they are trapped under asphalt,
encased prisoners of the highway.
They want to break through into the light —
to breathe, to see again, to tell the stories
of how far they came.
The sign here indicates it's only
a short distance to St. Peter's Harbour.

Good Friday

A victim of
bloodlust
he hung like
a side of beef
trussed up —
a sign of
contradiction
to his age —
to our age.
Were you there?
we will be —
We look for
signs daily.
His was a
signature
for the ages
written into
history —
a testament.
The atrocities
of our times
are strung
up with him —
we are there.

A Lamentation for Nicaragua and Honduras

This day the unplanned chain of tragedy
solidifies into history.
For years it was machine guns and machetes
in place of flowers.
Revolution: the irascible line of their fate.

Next, uncontrolled wind sweeps over their
sugar and banana plantations
and violence hurls up in towering waves.
The fruit of the summer withers
in the shriek of the wind,
and rain-hammered hilltops cascade
like lava over their huts:
the gardens dying, the gardens a graveyard.

Later, under a still alien sky
their cries fall like stones.
A mother wails, trembling, praying, imploring
for her bloodchild under the mire.
In this night of despair
even the bread of life is bitter.
The wings of madness hover over the fathers
as they wade through the sludge —
under the weight of the living —
in search of 10,000 engravings in the mud.

Our souls burn away with sympathy
for our brothers and sisters in pain.
Fifty years, they say it will take,
until the rough landscape will rise again.

Metamorphosis

The tragic death of ones so young is cause
for more grief than a body can hold. Such
were the losses of Patricia and La Quinta
in separate accidents. Yet, their spirits return.
To make grief bearable? Who can answer?

Was it promises unfulfilled
that brought them back?
One, a butterfly settling on
the mother's hand as she tends
her amazing garden,
flying a short distance,
returning, returning daily,
resettling, its delicate wings
caressing fingers.
The other, on her funeral day,
a bluejay tending her
fledgling chick, fallen
from a high branch —
unable to fly, so young.
The mother perching on the deck
refusing to fly off when shooed,
watching her baby take refuge
in a flowerbed before being
run over in the neighbour's

driveway. She, swooping down,
leaving a blue feather,
now a bookmark, a daily
reminder of beautiful grief.
Each visit unfolds
another consoling memory
of angels in flight.
Next year, their footprints
will bloom into roses.

The Day the Tree Came Down

The tall spruce by the driveway had to come down.
A huge battered thing, it was rotten at the heart.
Still, it was a part of our children's world.
At bedtime stories it was their hop-off to the moon.
They rode its crescent to the galaxies of the stars, to wild Orion's lair,
to bring a little dipper of treats to the Great Bear.

There was a threat it might topple down upon our house
in a strong southwesterly. "It just has to come down,"
you said. "How to fell it is the question," I said.
"There's enough space between it and the barn."
"But if it should take it into its mind to fall
another way?"

They came with their chain saw.
Son Daniel, the climber, scaled
the tree to the top to secure a long, long rope, and
Frank Gallant began sawing through the trunk,
first notching it in the direction we were to pull.
The trunk resisted, the tree of knowledge having its
final say. The saw, too hot, went into a stall —
snagged on fence wire embedded there for years.
A new set of teeth, then back to work.

The family took tension on the rope.
The tree came crashing down to quake the ground
to the predetermined spot just inches from the barn —
a felled skyscraper. That night, despite our fears
it might, the sky did not fall. It sagged,
but not enough to make the moon our vehicle to the stars.

Early March, 2006

After a mild winter, spring comes as no surprise,
the sap fooled in February rose
in the sugar maples; the Canada
geese in fact never left, the grain

fields laid bare for their foragers' daily diet. Beware,
there is familiar danger in this,
St. Patrick's Day will call
back the white assassin

with mounds of snow and winds
to wake the dead of Lent till Good Friday.
The crocuses, spring's harbingers, will
creep back under their blankets.

Farmers will greet the flaky torrent, the poor
man's fertilizer promises a better
crop year; while bugs object, shivering
in their larval cocoons.
Yet the scent of spring will not be denied,
Celsius cannot stem its rising trend;
our own awakening from winter sleep
will draw back the curtains to the slanting sun.

The Bonshaw Hills

Thanksgiving weekend draws us to the Bonshaw Hills,
an annual observance as sure as harvest time.
We park our car on the narrow roadside cathedral'd in the trees —
step out to feel the cool red soil under foot and to inhale
the aroma of nature preparing its falling compost bed:
a mosaic of leaves strewn at the foot of an aged beech,
the distilled yellow hues of birch, the frilly oak.
The muffle of a soft-landing acorn, the scurry of squirrels.

We drop in on a pipe-connected sugar maple stand,
at rest until next spring's sap run, and come upon
a red maple like glowing embers among the pines and firs.
We climb to the hill's highest point to catch the full
autumn symphony in the valleys below. Then, after dusk,
by foot memory we find our way back to our car:
a colour-chronicle for a winter's night
when all the world goes black and white.

Thoughts Taken at Greenwich

If I had yet a life to live
I'd spend it going about declaring wildernesses
such as the lower end of Greenwich's peninsula —
just beyond where Jack Gab's farm used to be
before the sands overran it,
in the days when the wilderness overtook humanity
rather than the other way around.

We spend this Saturday there at Greenwich,
wife, family, and self:
the children flit over the dunes like sandpipers —
hardly leaving a track. Wife snapshoots
snaggle-toothed tree stumps protruding
like runic characters against the grey fall sky.
"Look there," I say, as a marsh hawk sweeps
and dives to make its kill; the morsel field mouse
surely does not break nature's balance.

"Try not to walk on the marram grass!"
an echo from our ecological daughter
studying on another continent. "If you step
on a plant five times, you kill it."
We obey her voice of conscience,
preoccupied with the moral law within
and God's delicate world without. A son
rescues an offspring salamander deserted

in the sands. The warmth and dampness of his
cupped hands nurse its encrusted body back
to life before releasing it in Schooner Pond.

And, what d'y'know, an oasis cranberry patch
in one of the dune valleys closest to the Gulf shore.
We fill our pockets with rich red berries for sauce
for supper. This ritual act makes communion
with all those other species for whom
Greenwich is home and provider.
This is an enduring creation. We regard it with awe.

The Red Dirt Road

Not by design, the red dirt road evolved:
horse trails bringing mail and goods to rural folks,
or else cow paths. The red dirt road is communal.
It is half road and half landscape.
A winding brook beside lays out its course;
a solid maple is in the way; it goes around it.
It can be as narrow as it likes: not a triumph
over nature but a concurrence.

A ruddy etching between wilderness and civilization,
in summer it invites to be strolled; notice
shy trilliums, ubiquitous Queen Anne's lace,
rare lady's slipper, birches, fir, mountain ash.
In winter, it's for trudging.
In a downpour, it's one long trough.
Custodian of the antique, it's unfriendly to cars,
slowing progress in the curling lip of a rut.
The red dirt road was here first,
and it will endure.

Confederation Trail

Take the northwest footpath out of town
and in no time
you'll be walking on the trail.
Here you can set the mind's cares
down among the spruces in the shadows
and let your eyes graze
on daisies thick as constellations
on the trailside's russet haze
and on the blossoming clover that blankets
the adjacent field.
Soon it will be mowed for hay
but now it's yours
to take what consolation you may.

Red Fox

Her silver cousins once a boon
to this Island's economy, now past,
the land's left to the free-range red fox.
Clairvoyant and hunter-lean
she darts like a sleek sleuth
across the fresh-snowed field
following a line of rabbit tracks,
her prize a patch of blood
and two long, mitteny white ears —
another case solved, she's best at survival.

She has no starved look but, when
the hunt bears no unriddling,
she pilfers suet from our bird feeders,
eats garbage without relish, mice.
In spring, we panic over missing chicks.
When we catch a glimpse of her eyes,
she's more cunning than last year's
raccoon we trapped in the coop.

Island Skies, a song

In the west, a waning moon goes down,
Sweeping back over the headland.
And the tide comes home to the harbour,
And the tide comes home to me.

I hope the moon shines for you in your far country,
But the skies there are not Island skies.
Where you are out of reach of the sea,
Where you are away from me.

Tonight I'm restless in the wind;
The rain is salty from the sea.
And white breakers roll inland in the dark.
This is where I want to be.

The trouble in me rolls out on the wind to you.
It rides on the crest of the moon.
Will you remember the salt smell of the sea?
Will you remember me?

Tonight I'm restless in the wind;
The rain is salty from the sea.
And white breakers roll inland in the dark.
This is where I want to be.
This is where I want to be.

Go to the Sea

"Go to the sea!" "Go to the sea!" The books of my boyhood said to me.
Being Islanders, we are wedded to the sea.
We watch waves roll in from the edge of the earth, speculate about their origin.
They come with coded messages from beyond the horizon,
betimes messages of peace and serenity on rippling surfaces,
and at other times as raging foreboding on foaming waves.

As we break out of the cove and pass beyond the headland,
gulls follow our ship almost without moving their wings.
We celebrate their company by contributing portions of our food.
They break out into a fire of white wings and dive down to the waves,
the seascape around us awhirl as they pluck the manna of scraps.

Suddenly, they dive down to the sea and are gone and we are alone
with a horizon that appears always and ever to outreach our grasp.
Still we strive on towards it. Our voyage has a beginning but no end.
This is how we pursue it, its fleeting promise like the odyssey for eternity.
This is the sea in which all cries are hushed. Without space there is
neither innocence nor liberty.

It is already noon, and we sail onward and outward. As we do,
the waves cut against our bow. The water scatters into shapes that die
and are reborn in our wake. Each wave brings its distinctive promise.

It is true, other ships come into sight, but as soon as they appear,
they disappear in the silence. What person who cherishes the sea
and its loneliness can ever stop loving others who share the same destiny?

A little later still, the moon begins its ascent to the sky.
At its zenith, it lays down its own special message in a narrow,
white corridor on the water's surface. It is a message of light to the darkness.
At the same instant, the wind lets up completely. We heave to,
cut our engine, and meditate on the amicable water
in its serene rise and fall, lulling into reverie.

In the following morning, the cool water gently under our propeller.
Towards noon we are well on our way back to land.
Then, as evening approaches, we near the lukewarm shore.
Rather than the disappointment of not achieving answers beyond the horizon,
we are filled with satisfaction about our launching forth,
about the thought which transfigures, a decisive act, a great work,
an irresistible quest. Living like this is the delicious anguish of being.

We drop anchor in the bay now populated by many other boats.
We swim ashore. It is just beyond twilight, but the sand is still warm.
The birds have gone to rest. All that is left to us, even here, is space and time.

Passages

I am no more than a droplet in the stream of life.
Life goes on around me. I see it flow like a river in slow motion.
I am a part of it, of every small wave and ripple spending itself
on the bank. Sometimes I get caught up in currents
I cannot control, and sometimes I get thrown violently onto a rock,
then swept back into the foaming rush to be bounced about
like a kayak in white water.

Other times the flow is as slow as time, and as I ride along
on the surface waters, I can see the bottom clearly
through the steady currents that run under me.
Sometimes I can count every pebble in the river bed,
and every small trout speckle,
with the clarity of truth. Sometimes there is not movement at all,
a seeming perfect stillness. But to this I cannot say: "This is
where I belong. I will stay here. I will do the work of my life here."

The pull of the current leads me on.
My destination, as inevitable as the end of life itself,
is the ocean in all its immensity.
There I am called to the marvel of survival
under the pounding of waves and the flow of tides,
flavoured by the sometimes bitter, sometimes savoury salt.

I am a privileged droplet. I have the opportunity and the
challenge eventually to get to the great ocean.

I could as easily have ended up in someone's septic tank or have been zonked by
pollution in the lagoon of an industrial waste.
Larger bodies of water along the way say to me:
"But you're nothing more than a molecule.
What significance can you possibly have?
Wait till you get to the ocean; you will
appear even smaller in that vast body of water.
What can you expect to do then?" Fear tells me how easy it would be
to splash upon a rock and stay there, and evaporate in the sun,
or to join some of my acquaintances who've left the stream to
escape into a stagnant pool along the way. "Don't get
involved," they warn. "The risks are too high."

Still, knowing that all tides turn and all tides return
to those who are strong enough to face them,
I do not fear whatever lies beyond my power, not even what lurks
in the darkest reaches of my journey. For I am given
this moment to dream dreams and to implant goals
for my future. Do not ask me, precisely, what
that future will be; simply be assured that it will be.
This is the vision my secret eyes reveal to me.
What I can see for the moment is enough to keep me going.

Insight

Miniature pictures of God catch our eyes
and hold them spellbound:
a blade of grass etching the wind,
a firefly flicker, a dewy spider web
at sunrise, hummingbird's wings, a speckled
trout's sudden flash in the shallows,
a pair of beguiling eyelashes,
things we catch at a glance
out of the corner of our eye —
something twitching and bright —
mirrors flashing back Divine beauty,
glad surprises to break the tedium
of our daily execution of cosmic chores —
a stay against the glare of the city's golden mile.
Our language breaks down before
the splendour of the infinite.
A glimpse of the truth is all we have,
searching for enlightenment among hidden things.

Being a Christian

At its heart lies an approach
to the spiritual, its centre the transcendence
and unity of personal experiences,
the arbiter of truth, a deep core
that surpasses self and time
when morality is not an end but a means.

Its vision stands independent of doctrine,
of edict, canon, inquisition, politics,
and is immune to the winds of change.

It is a reflection of humanity
carrying within it the hopes,
dreams, and nightmares of the human spirit —
its great triumphs and great failures.

Postscript

From the open boundaries of inquiry
I can still hear the urgent echo
of the thinker and teacher — testing
the limits of the unimaginable and the unavoidable,
chasing down ideas to the real, or seeming so.
Shackled to the mood and condition of my time,
I cannot remain content with half-knowledge —
resist the temptation to a despairing shrug —
push on with the uncompromising quest,
leaving no room for hesitation or timidity.

Bowed but unbent by retirement, though
awarded the headstone carving, "emeritus" —
a small credit for a subdued reputation—
not celebrated for aesthetic rhapsody,
I continue to press forward with intuition,
strumming the tumultuous strain
that sustains the symphony of being —
not the relic of a career terminated,
but an inexorable postscript.

Late October

This falling I can hear:
the solitude of one leaf's
reluctance to go. Close your eyes
and you can hear it, too:
a single cricket's final cry,
the blackbirds parliamenting
in the trees and, at the shore,
the acoustics of water lapping.

Boys stash away vacation bikes;
girls, sandals-shorts-halters.
Evening goes down like stage lights,
but, later, stars twinkle brighter
in the crisp air; geese track south
across the moon; asters, the last flowers
to bid adieu; potato crops rise from their
roots to greet the killing frost.

The ground is littered, holding
our memories in layers of leaves,
our eyes turning them like pages
to times when our own yearnings
loosened and fell, leaf by leaf. Someone
from the shadows comes and goes.
We will read and write letters
until the last leaf blows away.
The light now is sharper, if less.

The O.R.

This laſt, to say a word,
Utter a sentence, work up a smile
For all those masked assurances.
I take the life-releasing needle —
Strapped into capital punishment's gurney —
Before anaeſthetic oblivion
Clamps on the lid of silence.

Three hours later, coming out of fog,
I discover a confident calm
And decide to take up life anew.
I will turn my craft to leeward
And avoid the sea ſtorms hereafter.
Thou shalt not be killed, a new commandment.
Today I can walk on water.

Winter Walk

My boots grind out their crunch,
with each step an age passes —
another year in my ascent.
My knees knock the days, the years
slip by, icing over.

Inside, my wife is icing a dark
cake, humming Lightfoot.
The snow eddies outside her window
so she cannot see my trudge
back across the yard.

As the door falls open, heat's
breath overtakes the nippy air
and draws me rejuvenated
into her warm presence. Years
melt off my arctic boots.

Tranquility

When our children have gone at last,
we'll go and live by the ocean shore
on the far side of the lake. We'll cock our
ears to catch the surf's crashing against
the dunes. Whenever the wind howls and
our electricity fails, as it surely will,
our kerosene lamp will make a globe
around our narrow space. We'll wage war
at cards until the tide's retreating — its
trumps all played out — draws us back
to serenity. I will be old, you still young,
or relatively so. We'll munch on mussels
and dulse to keep healthy, and crush
lobster shells to fertilize our flower patch.
We'll count the time that's left to us
from day to day — not years. We'll stay
till the time must come for us to cross.

Shades of Light

...leaning my forehead against the cool glass, I looked over at the dark house where she lived. I may have stood there for an hour, seeing nothing but the brown-clad figure cast by my imagination, touched discreetly by the lamplight at the curved neck, at the hand upon the railings and the border below the skirt.

— James Joyce, "Araby"

The best light is a shaft.
The Dutch masters knew how well
it played upon a scene, cutting sideways
from an adjacent window or lamp,
bringing balance between light and shadow
to give a deeper vision. Or the scant
outline of Mangan's sister's curved neck,
hand and hem invoking the full dimension —
my students' dream girl — more carnal
to the imagination than a centrefold.
"Heard melodies are sweet, but those unheard
are sweeter," comes back to mind from those
classroom days.

The flash and glare of light is too much
with us now, the dazzle of it, exciting
action and passion, the laser play;
the cruel painter, photoluminescent on the
screen or page. Rather, give me the slanting
light of dawn or dusk, the rising sun
by pools of stillness, the pleasure of spruce

hedgerows at its setting, and how those polar
shadows make the vertical work more stately.
Give me an Island woman crosslit at sunset,
her hair shorewind blown, her skirts awry,
on her face the horizon's full glow:
her seagirt hereness, a signature.

Acknowledgments

This collection of poems is in most ways my thank you and acknowledgment of my being appointed the Island's Poet Laureate in 2004. I have read selections of these poems to several receptive audiences, so a book seemed appropriate.

I thank our Island and its "spirit of place," first and foremost, for its abiding inspiration. I am also in debt to my wife, Carolyn, and our family: Jane and Stephen, Patrick and Tara, Emily, Thomas and Isabelle, Daniel, and Christian. They are my first readers and critics.

I owe a special gratitude to Jane for her professionalism in editing and shaping the poems, to Danny for his cover painting of *The Taste of Water*, to Matthew MacKay for the book's welcoming design, and to Laurie Brinklow and her Acorn Press, for her continuing support and commitment to Island literature.

About the painting

The Taste of Water [40 x 50 cm], oil on canvas by Danny Ledwell.

Danny Ledwell is a graduate of Mount Allison University's Fine Arts program. His paintings can be found in private collections around the Maritimes and beyond.